J B Ziegle
Pelleschi, Andrea, 1962-
Maddie Ziegler /
$7.95        on1108788393

W9-AKD-214
3 4028 10549 1554
HARRIS COUNTY PUBLIC LIBRARY

BRIGHT
IDEA
BOOKS

# MADDIE
# Ziegler

by Andrea Pelleschi

DISCARD

CAPSTONE PRESS
a capstone imprint

Bright Ideas is published by Capstone Press, an imprint of Capstone.
1710 Roe Crest Drive
North Mankato, Minnesota 56003
www.capstonepub.com

Copyright © 2020 by Capstone. All rights reserved. No part of this publication may be reproduced in whole or in part, or stored in a retrieval system, or transmitted in any form or by any means, electronic, mechanical, photocopying, recording, or otherwise, without written permission of the publisher.

**Library of Congress Cataloging-in-Publication Data**
Names: Pelleschi, Andrea, 1962- author.
Title: Maddie Ziegler / by Andrea Pelleschi.
Description: North Mankato, MN : Capstone Press, 2020. | Series: Influential People | Includes
    index. | Audience: Grades 4-6
Identifiers: LCCN 2019029524 (print) | LCCN 2019029525 (ebook) | ISBN 9781543590784
(hardcover) | ISBN 9781496665867 (paperback) | ISBN 9781543590791 (ebook)
Subjects: LCSH: Ziegler, Maddie—Juvenile literature. | Child dancers—United States—Biography. |
    Dancers—United States--Biography--Juvenile literature.
Classification: LCC GV1785.Z56 P45 2020  (print) | LCC GV1785.Z56  (ebook) |
DDC 792.802/8092 [B]—dc23
LC record available at https://lccn.loc.gov/2019029524
LC ebook record available at https://lccn.loc.gov/2019029525

**Image Credits**
Alamy: WENN Rights Ltd, 27; AP Images: Lionel Hahn/Abaca/Sipa USA, cover; iStockphoto:
FatCamera, 30–31; Newscom: Jen Lowery/Splash News, 12; Rex Features: Broadimage, 9, 11,
David Buchan, 23, Gregory Pace, 21, Joe Papeo, 5; Shutterstock Images: Dfree, 15, Featureflash
Photo Agency, 18, 24, Kathy Hutchins, 17, 29, Tinseltown, 6, 28
Design Elements: Shutterstock Images

**Editorial Credits**
Editor: Charly Haley; Designer: Laura Graphenteen; Production Specialist: Colleen McLaren

All internet sites appearing in back matter were available and accurate when this book was sent to press.

Printed in the United States of America.
PA99

# TABLE OF CONTENTS

# CHAPTER 1

# BIG Break

Maddie Ziegler danced in a music video in 2014. It was for pop star Sia. The name of the song was "Chandelier." The video was Maddie's big break.

# MEETING SIA

Sia had first seen Maddie on a TV show called *Dance Moms*. Sia thought Maddie was a very **talented** dancer. She asked Maddie to be in her video. Maddie was just 11 years old.

Maddie Ziegler danced onstage as Sia sang in 2016.

Maddie became more famous after working with Sia.

6

# BIG HIT

Maddie's dance in the video was strange. She wore a white wig. She made faces. People around the world noticed her.

"Chandelier" became a big hit. When Sia sang it on TV, Maddie danced by her.

## WATCHING "CHANDELIER"

People have watched the "Chandelier" video more than 2 billion times.

Sia asked Maddie to be in four more videos. She brought Maddie on tour with her. They became close friends.

Working with Sia gave Maddie many opportunities. Maddie likes to dance and act. She also writes and models. She has even worked on a movie with Sia.

Maddie (left) and Sia (right) sometimes wear matching outfits.

# CHAPTER 2

# BORN TO
# Dance

Maddie was born in Pittsburgh, Pennsylvania. She started dancing when she was 2 years old.

Maddie joined the Abby Lee Dance Company when she was 4 years old. At first Maddie danced in the back row. But she practiced a lot. She worked hard. Soon her teachers moved her to the first row.

Maddie began dancing when she was young.

Maddie at the Teen Choice Awards in 2012

Maddie started dance **competitions** a year later. She won her first **trophy** at age 6. After that, she won many more awards.

## PRACTICE MAKES PERFECT

**Maddie works hard. She tries to make each dance perfect. She sometimes spends more than 30 hours a week practicing dance.**

## DANCE MOMS

In 2011 Maddie joined a TV show. It was called *Dance Moms*. She was 8 years old. The show was about girls who dance. It was also about their mothers. Maddie's sister and mother were also on the show. They stayed on *Dance Moms* for five years. Maddie had been on the show for three years when Sia first saw her.

Maddie (second from left) with other dancers from *Dance Moms*

# CHAPTER 3

# MORE THAN
# Dancing

Maddie liked being on *Dance Moms*. But she wanted to try new things. Sia's videos brought new opportunities for her.

# WRITING

Maddie wrote a book about her life. It was called *The Maddie Diaries*. It came out in 2017 and was a **best seller**. She also wrote three novels. They are about a dancer named Harper. The third one came out in 2019.

*The Maddie Diaries* was Maddie's first book.

Acting has helped Maddie become even more famous.

18

## ACTING

Maddie was herself on *Dance Moms*. But she has acted as **characters** on other TV shows. She acted in her first show in 2012. She has also acted in movies. One of them was called *Leap!* It came out in 2016. It was an **animated** film. Maddie used only her voice. She played a ballerina.

In 2017 Maddie filmed a movie with Sia called *Music*. Maddie played the main character. Sia directed the movie. Sia worked on the movie for a couple of years.

# MODELING AND FASHION

Maddie models clothes and makeup. She has been on many magazine covers. In 2016 she started her own fashion line called *MADDIE*.

## INSTAGRAM FOLLOWERS

Maddie posts many photos of herself on Instagram. She has more than 13 million followers.

Maddie (left) at a fashion show with actresses Joey King and Olivia Holt

21

# CHAPTER 4

# GIVING
# Back

Maddie likes giving back to other people. She often works with her sister Mackenzie. They visited sick children for the Starlight Children's **Foundation** in 2012. They asked people to make birthday cards in 2016. The cards were for homeless children.

Maddie spoke at a charity event in 2018.

Maddie (left) and her sister support groups that help people who have cancer.

# OTHER CAUSES

In 2016 Maddie danced at a special party called a gala. The party raised money for the Dizzy Feet Foundation. That group helps give dance education to people who cannot afford it.

In 2018 Maddie and Mackenzie made a video for Dancers Against Cancer. This group gives money to help dancers who are sick with cancer.

# WORKING WITH SIA

Maddie and Sia have worked to help people with AIDS. People with AIDS get very sick. In 2018 Maddie and Sia raised money to help. They made an ad to sell Sia's brand of lipstick. Maddie wore red lipstick in the ad. Sia's song "Helium" was in the ad too. The lipstick sales went to an AIDS fund.

Maddie is busy with many things. She dances a lot. She acts and models too. She writes books. But Maddie finds time to give back to others. With so many talents, Maddie has a bright future.

Sia (left), who is known for not showing her face, keeps working with Maddie.

# GLOSSARY

**animated**
in the form of a cartoon

**best seller**
a book that sells better than similar books

**character**
an imaginary person played by an actor in a TV show or movie

**competition**
a contest in which people show what they can do, like dancing, to see who is best

**foundation**
an organization that raises money for a good cause

**talent**
something a person is naturally good at

**trophy**
an award or prize

# TIMELINE

**2002:** Maddie Ziegler is born on September 30.

**2004:** Maddie begins dance lessons.

**2011:** Maddie joins *Dance Moms*.

**2014:** Maddie dances in Sia's music video "Chandelier."

**2017:** Maddie writes *The Maddie Diaries*.

**2018:** Maddie and Sia work together to raise money for people with AIDS.

# ACTIVITY

## CREATE A DANCE

Maddie has done all kinds of dancing. Create your own dance! Find a song you like. Make up moves for the song. Put them all together into a dance. Be as creative as you want. Invite your friends to join you. You can even film your dance like a music video.

Harris County Public Library
Houston, Texas

# FURTHER RESOURCES

## Want to learn more about Maddie Ziegler?
## Check out these resources:

Maddie and Mackenzie Ziegler's Official Website:
http://www.thezieglergirls.com

Ziegler, Maddie. *The Maddie Diaries*. New York: Simon & Schuster, 2017.

## Interested in learning more about dancers?
## Read these books:

Bell, Samantha S. *You Can Work in Dance*. North Mankato, Minn.: Capstone Press, 2019.

Golkar, Golriz. *Misty Copeland*. North Mankato, Minn.: Capstone Press, 2019.

Van der Linde, Laurel. *So, You Want to Be a Dancer?: The Ultimate Guide to Exploring the Dance Industry*. Hillsboro, Ore.: Beyond Words, 2015.

# INDEX

7